The Manager's Pocket Guide to
RECRUITING THE WORKFORCE OF THE FUTURE

Bruce Tulgan

HRD PRESS
Amherst, Massachusetts

LAKEWOOD PUBLICATIONS
Minneapolis, Minnesota

© 1998 by Bruce Tulgan

Published by:

HRD Press
22 Amherst Road
Amherst, MA 01002
1-800-822-2801
413-253-3490 (fax)
www.hrdpress.com

Lakewood Publications
50 South Ninth Street
Minneapolis, MN 55402
1-800-707-7769
612-340-4819 (fax)
www.trainingsupersite.com

PRINTED IN CANADA

ISBN 0-87425-433-7

Cover design by Eileen Klockars
Editorial services by Mary George

TABLE OF CONTENTS

Table of Contents

PART 3   Selecting the Stars of the Workforce of the Future

INTRODUCTION

Unemployment clings to record lows, and competition for skilled workers is almost as fierce as competition for customers. Recruiting the best of the labor pool is serious business in today's economy.

Companies need flexible, technoliterate, information-savvy workers who think like entrepreneurs, take charge of their own careers, and stand ready to adapt themselves to ever changing roles and responsibilities. The irony is, the workers who best fit this profile are the very same young workers whom business leaders have decried, in survey after survey, as disloyal "slackers" who have short attention spans, don't want to be told what to do, and can't stand deferred gratification. As it turns out, the "slacker" stereotype and the "worker of the future" profile are like mirror images of each other; thus companies in every industry are now scrambling to recruit the best young talent.

However, recruiting can become an agonizing process when new employees continually turn over before adding at least as much value as the cost of recruiting and training them. As skilled workers of all ages trade security for mobility, young workers are leading the charge, moving from one company to the next, soaking up training resources, relationships with decision makers, and proof of their ability to add value.

During the early waves of downsizing, restructuring, and reengineering, business leaders tried to wean workers off their outdated career expectations. But, in contrast to older workers, most younger workers never had time to consider the old-fashioned career path (pay your dues; climb the ladder), much less mourn its loss.

Now we young people have an answer for all those folks who keep asking us, "Are you ever going to get a job?" The answer, once and for all, is "We're in business for ourselves." As put by a thirty-year-old MBA student with consulting experience in firms both large and small:

> *Get a job? Whatever. I like to think of myself more as an independent contractor: Work hard on a project, cash out, then reassess and renegotiate.*

It may be an accident of history, but younger workers are starting their working lives during the most profound changes in the nature of work since the industrial revolution.

The old-fashioned job is just too stodgy for today's

fast-moving markets, fierce competition, and unpre-dictable staffing needs. That's why companies are redesigning everything about the way work gets done.

They are dissolving old-fashioned departments and bringing people and resources together along product and services lines or in ad hoc teams that address immediate needs. Work systems, which in some cases have been in place for decades, are being dismantled and refashioned to improve flexibility, efficiency, and effectiveness.

Organizations are also leveling out their hierarchies and making way for fluid cross-trained teams that tackle whatever work needs to be done. Workers who remain as part of "right-sized" core groups of perma-nent employees (those in the organization for more than three years) must be prepared to work in project teams alongside temps, consultants, outsource workers, and short-termers.

Of course, even if the old-fashioned job is dead, there is still a lot of work to be done. But work relation-ships can no longer be based on dues paying for job security. Rather, employees and employers must shape short-term, win-win arrangements in which workers contribute their skills and energies to create tangible results in exchange for financial and non-financial compensation and incentives.

The Challenge for Workers

As workers of the future, young people must become the sole proprietors of our own skills and abilities, regardless of whether we work in what looks like a traditional "job," or are temps or consultants, or are launching our own small businesses. No matter where we go, no matter what we do, we truly are in business for ourselves. We will need to take charge of our lives and careers, look for self-building dividends in each new experience, adapt to constantly changing circumstances, stay flexible, and keep building from within so we become more and more valuable in the increasingly free and fluid labor market.

The Challenge for Employers

The challenge for every employer is to turn a potential staffing crisis into a powerful strategic advantage by becoming the employer of choice for the workforce of the future. As such, your organization will attract the best people and keep them longer. Instead of watching your recruiting and training dollars go walking out the door, you will reap greater dividends on that investment and possibly become a magnet for the recruiting and training investments of your competitors.

What You Will Find in this Pocket Guide

This pocket guide is divided into three parts corresponding to the three phases of recruiting: (1) profiling the people you want to hire, (2) running a campaign to attract a large, diverse pool of applicants who fit the profile, and (3) selecting the stars.

Part 1, profiling, revolves around thirty-one skills to look for in workers of the future. The guide discards obsolete criteria from the workplace of the past, suggests a broad profile of the Generation X worker, and provides a profile building tool that will help you create a clear, skill-focused profile of the kind of applicant most suitable for the position you are seeking to fill.

Part 2 gives you a full collection of tools for completing the planning stages of your recruiting campaign, including goal setting, message development, resource planning, and scheduling.

Part 3, selection, will help you update your selection process to focus on gathering proof that applicants have the skills you are looking for. Four methods are recommended, complete with tools and suggestions for carrying them out.

PROFILING THE WORKERS
OF THE FUTURE

Before you start an all-out recruiting campaign, it is important to profile exactly what kind of applicant you hope to attract. If you can target the ideal applicant with precision, then later, when it comes time to run your campaign, you will be able to develop a more persuasive recruiting message and concentrate greater resources on delivering the message to that much smaller target group.

Profiling is also essential to the selection process. If you have given thorough attention to profile building, your selection work will be clear-cut: to find the applicant who best fits the profile.

Profile of the Worker of the Future

Today's young workers are Generation X. Generation X has become the ubiquitous referent for my generation—the 52 million Americans born between 1963 and 1977.

Xers grew up in the aftermath of the baby boomers' discrediting of institutions, when society's most important institutions were faltering—schools, cities, government, big business, traditional religions. As Xers began entering the workforce, big business went through downsizing and reengineering; thus Xers clearly know that the old-time workplace bargain—dues paying and loyalty for security—is obsolete.

> *Face it. You're on your own. That's the way I look at it. And that's cool. I'm pretty comfortable with that. I have no doubt about my ability to succeed.*
>
> — Salesperson in an office-furniture dealership, age 24

Xers are used to a short-term world in which nothing is certain. That is why they are always looking for the day-to-day dividends on any investment of their only career capital—time, labor, and creativity. Xers are flexible and ready to reinvent themselves and their roles in any organization.

> *My boss told me, "Don't ever quit on me without coming to talk to me about it first." . . . Two months ago, I was looking for another job, and I went in to talk with him about it. We talked about some opportunities inside the company, and he was really open to getting me in front of more challenges. So I'm still here.*
>
> — Associate producer for a television news organization, age 28. Had worked in the guest booking office; previously was an administrative assistant in an ad firm.

Xers tend to be information-savvy and technoliterate. People of all ages have experienced the information revolution, but it has actually shaped the way Xers think, learn, and communicate. They love to sort through and digest massive quantities of information at a fast pace, and know how to use technology to achieve that. Their natural inclination toward multiple focus (homework, remote control, telephone) and selective elimination ("Is this material going to be on the test?") makes them well suited to deal with the tidal wave of information and technology under which everyone in our society lives.

> *Not everybody can keep track of fifteen things at once,
> the way I can, which is an advantage for me. Some-
> times people will be talking with me and then stop and
> act as if I am not paying any attention to them. But I'll
> look up and say, "Keep going, I'm with you." Just
> because I'm not looking at you doesn't mean I'm not
> listening. I don't have time to do one thing at a time.*
>
> — Department team leader in a retail
> store, age 27. Has worked in
> several retail organizations; also
> as a temp.

We Xers are eager to prove ourselves by achieving
tangible results in our own way and on our own time.
Most of us spent a lot of time alone as children. Our
parents were more likely to be divorced, to both work,
or at least to be more permissive than parents of prior
generations. This background is what makes Xers
such independent problem solvers and is probably
why Xers are the most entrepreneurial new
generation of workers since the industrial revolution.

> *I like to do things my own way. That doesn't mean I
> can't work for someone else. It just means, you know,
> give me the space to prove what I can do, and once you
> see what I can do, get out of my way and let me do it.*
>
> — Analyst in an investment bank, age 25

Since Xers can remember, they have lived in a world where everything changes faster than anyone can keep track of. They have learned to monitor results aggressively—to seek regular feedback and check what is working and what is not—and to guide the process of ongoing change. Raised in a culture of immediacy and uncertainty, Xers expect the world to respond quickly to their output.

> *This guy I work with said in a peer review that I am always checking to see where I stand. That's all that matters to me. I want to know where I stand. . . . I do check frequently. You never know, you know?*
>
> — Research assistant in a nonprofit organization, age 23

In short, we can profile Generation Xers in the following way.

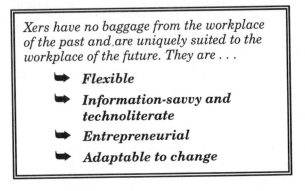

Xers have no baggage from the workplace of the past and are uniquely suited to the workplace of the future. They are . . .

➡ *Flexible*

➡ *Information-savvy and technoliterate*

➡ *Entrepreneurial*

➡ *Adaptable to change*

This is precisely the kind of worker that every management expert and every business leader has been saying organizations are going to need to compete and succeed in our changing economy. The Generation X worker is the worker of the future.

Obsolete Criteria

Long-term loyalty, dues paying, and strict adherence to the chain of command are no longer the most important characteristics to look for in a new employee. In fact, such characteristics may not even be desirable in the "post-jobs era."

To find the best young workers today, you will need to discard many obsolete assumptions. For example, job-hoppers may be among the most flexible and adaptable workers you could find, so don't count them out. And be careful about dismissing applicants who seem to have short attention spans: they may also be the most comfortable with new technologies.

If you are looking for an original thinker with a strong entrepreneurial spirit, it might be wise to look for an applicant with a good old-fashioned "attitude problem." Finally, people who demand tons of feedback and immediate gratification are likely to be the ones most tuned in to today's accelerating pace of change.

Thirty-One Skills to Look for in Workers of the Future

While some traditional type of credentials may still be important for certain positions, most crucial in all workers of the future will be their learning practices, relationship skills, ability to identify and seize opportunities to add value, and readiness to adapt in an environment of constant change. Let's take a closer look at these four categories and their skill sets.

LEARNING

1. **Voracious learning.** The desire to devour and process information rapidly, get up to speed on new skills and knowledge, and stay ahead of the rapidly accelerating obsolescence curve.

2. **Multiple focus.** The ability to juggle many different images, sounds, and texts coming from different sides all at once (dinner on one knee, homework on the other, remote control in one hand, telephone in the other . . . driving the market for call waiting).

3. **Strategic learning.** The ability to sort through today's vast tidal wave of information and make acute decisions about what one can discard and what one is going to learn.

4. **Information management.** The ability to frame research inquiries, effectively access information sources, gather worthwhile data, and understand, interpret, and think of valuable ways to use that data.

5. **Critical thinking.** The ability to differentiate between reliable and unreliable information, to carefully weigh the strengths of conflicting views,

and to make reasoned judgments. The habit of taking the time to consider possibilities, and not become attached to one point of view. Balancing an openness to others' views with independent judgment.

6. **Cultural literacy.** The desire and ability to master foreign languages and foreign cultures and to operate successfully in a global marketplace.

7. **Technoliteracy.** The desire and ability to learn and operate new technologies, particularly those related to computers and the World Wide Web.

8. **Being the diligent protégé of a worthy mentor.** Studying the example of an accomplished, experienced, wise person whom one admires.

RELATIONSHIPS

9. **Supply focus with respect to relationships.** Approaching relationships in terms of what one has to offer others, instead of what one needs or wants from others.

10. **Seeking out decision makers.** The ability to clarify the decisions that must be made to reach

particular goals, and then to identify the individuals who have the authority to make those decisions (or the influence to affect those decisions).

11. **Total customer service mindset.** Treating everyone like a valued customer—coworkers, employees, managers, suppliers, service people, as well as actual customers. Psyching out the needs of others and seeking to address them with cheerful promptness.

12. **Trustworthiness.** Spelling out clear expectations and assuming an absolute duty to fulfill those expectations. Being honest, realistic, responsible, on time, and accountable.

13. **Empathy.** The ability to imagine oneself in another person's position, and to tune in to the thoughts and feelings that person might have.

14. **Motivating others.** The ability to visualize positive results and enthusiastically share that positive vision in a way that inspires others.

15. **Facilitating the effectiveness of others.** The ability to train and coach others, set clear goals and deadlines, provide others with effective feedback, and reward good performance.

16. **Celebrating the success of others.** Giving people credit for their achievements, no matter how small, and trying to catch people doing things right.

17. **Being a mentor.** Helping another person learn and grow, and in the process, practicing one's leadership skills—priority setting, communication, and motivation.

18. **Communication.** The ability to listen (or to read) carefully and understand what others are thinking, feeling, and expressing; and the ability to speak (or to write) clearly and make oneself understood.

19. **Being a great team player.** The practice of sacrificing one's own autonomy and contributing one's best ideas and hardest work to pursue a shared purpose along with others; giving up some individual recognition in order to win recognition for the group and its shared purpose.

20. **Negotiation and conflict resolution.** The ability to clarify one's own bottom line, identify another's true bottom line, expose the common ground, and move oneself and another to that common ground.

VALUE ADDING

21. **Results focus.** The ability and inclination to organize one's work around clear, tangible goals and concrete deadlines.

22. **Identifying opportunities to add value.** The ability to identify problems others have not identified, problems others have not solved, services and products not yet invented, or services and products in need of improvement or delivery.

23. **Seizing opportunities to add value.** The ability to identify needs, match one's skills to those needs, define the value one is capable of adding, and then create an effective sales message to persuade decision makers to authorize and/or pay for the project.

24. **Deal closing.** The ability to clarify the parameters of a proposed transaction, identify the desired result of each party, move both parties to the common ground, eliminate mutually exclusive elements, and secure a binding agreement of both parties to execute the transaction.

25. **Strategic planning.** The ability to plan the achievement of goals by concrete deadlines, brainstorm available sources, map out intermediate goals and deadlines, and build a schedule of daily actions to meet each intermediate goal.

26. **Going the extra mile.** The practice of achieving more than one promises to achieve.

27. **Quality.** Holding oneself to a high standard. Thinking before speaking; outlining before writing (and always doing second drafts); planning before acting; double- and triple-checking before finalizing anything.

28. **Integrity.** A commitment to act on one's best knowledge and intentions; to be honest with oneself and with others, and to remain faithful to basic ethical principles.

ADAPTABILITY

29. **Gauging change.** The practice of monitoring feedback from every source to keep track of what is changing and what is staying the same, what is still working and what is no longer working.

30. **Flexibility.** The willingness and ability to continually make adjustments in one's goals, plans, and practices every step of the way as necessitated by changing circumstances.

31. **Adaptability.** The ability and willingness to learn new skills, perform new tasks, do old tasks in new ways, work with new machines, new managers, new coworkers, new customers, new rules, no rules; to do whatever is needed, whenever it's needed; to go, on any given day, from one boss to another, from one team to another, from one organization to another, from one set of tasks to another.

Profiling the Person You Want to Hire

When you are seeking to fill any position in any company in any industry, the ideal is to find lots of applicants who excel in all of the thirty-one skills and traits listed above. But you can't expect to recruit Wonder Woman or Superman for every position in every company in every industry. By the same token, don't fall into the common recruiting trap of hiring a very impressive person who, nonetheless, does not have the right mix of skills and traits to carry out the tasks and responsibilities of the position.

No matter how impressed you may be with a particular applicant, if the applicant's skills and traits do not match the position, you are looking at the wrong person. The German-speaking computer genius is splendid, but not necessarily for a customer service position in retail. The consummate deal closer who has also won the customer service award for five years running may still be the wrong person to manage a telephone call-center. And so on.

The key to profiling is to identify the skills and traits that are most important for a particular position, so you can seek applicants with the mix of strengths you need.

Using the Worker of the Future™ Profile Builder

Part 1 concludes with an easy-to-use tool that will help you build a clear, skill-focused profile of the kind of applicant most suitable for the position you are seeking to fill. The tool comprises three basic steps:

1. *Brainstorming the position to be filled.* This step focuses on clarifying basic recruiting issues such as why you are seeking to hire someone right now and what tasks, functions, and responsibilities you want the new employee to assume.

2. *Building the profile.* In Step 2, you will evaluate the importance of each of the Thirty-One Skills to Look for in Workers of the Future in relation to the position under consideration.

3. *Completing the profile.* Completion involves reviewing the evaluations, listing the essential and very important skills and traits for the position, and considering the issue of training.

By taking these three steps, you will create an indispensable profile to guide your further recruiting work for the position.

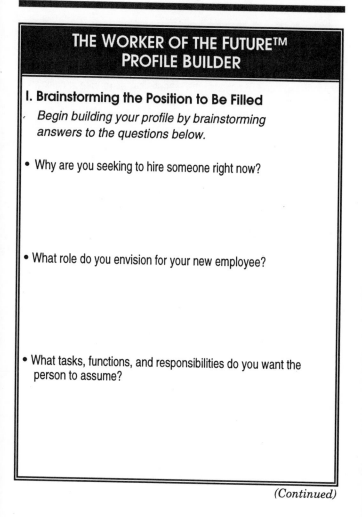

THE WORKER OF THE FUTURE™ PROFILE BUILDER

I. Brainstorming the Position to Be Filled

Begin building your profile by brainstorming answers to the questions below.

- Why are you seeking to hire someone right now?

- What role do you envision for your new employee?

- What tasks, functions, and responsibilities do you want the person to assume?

(Continued)

THE WORKER OF THE FUTURE™
PROFILE BUILDER (Continued)

- Do these tasks, functions, and responsibilities require specific skills and/or expertise? (If yes, what kind of skills? Do you need someone who already has the skills and/or expertise, or will your organization be training the person?)

- Is the position a high-contact position or low-contact? (Will the person often be interacting with others? If yes, describe those people, i.e., customers, vendors, coworkers, managers, etc.)

- Will the person have clear goals that remain fixed from day to day? Or is the work ad hoc and unpredictable?

(Continued)

THE WORKER OF THE FUTURE™
PROFILE BUILDER (Continued)

- Will the person be working regular hours, or are the hours irregular? Describe the kind of time commitment involved (long hours, short hours, a combination of both; predictable or hard to predict; seasonal; etc.).

- What are some of the hidden joys and rewards of the work the person will be doing?

- What are some of the hidden frustrations and difficulties of the work?

(Continued)

THE WORKER OF THE FUTURE™
PROFILE BUILDER (Continued)

II. Building the Profile

Keeping in mind the brainstorming you did in Step I, build a profile of the ideal worker for the job. Rate each of the Thirty-One Skills to Look for in Workers of the Future on its importance to the position you are seeking to fill.

Circle your answer, indicating whether the particular trait or skill is . . .

- (a) Absolutely necessary to the position
- (b) Very important to the position
- (c) Somewhat important to the position
- (d) Somewhat unimportant to the position
- (e) Totally unimportant to the position

---

1. **Voracious learning.** The desire and ability to devour and process information rapidly, get up to speed on new skills and knowledge, and stay ahead of the rapidly accelerating obsolescence curve.

   RATING: (a) (b) (c) (d) (e)

2. **Multiple focus.** The ability to juggle many different images, sounds, and texts coming from different sides all at once.

   RATING: (a) (b) (c) (d) (e)

(Continued)

THE WORKER OF THE FUTURE™
PROFILE BUILDER (Continued)

---

3. **Strategic learning.** The ability to sort through today's vast tidal wave of information and make acute decisions about what one can discard and what one is going to learn.

   RATING: (a)   (b)   (c)   (d)   (e)

4. **Information management.** The ability to frame research inquiries, effectively access information sources, gather worthwhile data, and understand, interpret, and think of valuable ways to use that data.

   RATING: (a)   (b)   (c)   (d)   (e)

5. **Critical thinking.** The ability to differentiate between reliable and unreliable information, to carefully weigh the strengths of conflicting views, and to make reasoned judgments. The habit of taking the time to consider possibilities, and not become attached to one point of view. Balancing an openness to others' views with independent judgment.

   RATING: (a)   (b)   (c)   (d)   (e)

6. **Cultural literacy.** The desire and ability to master foreign languages and foreign cultures and to operate successfully in a global marketplace.

   RATING: (a)   (b)   (c)   (d)   (e)

(Continued)

THE WORKER OF THE FUTURE™
PROFILE BUILDER (Continued)

7. **Technoliteracy.** The desire and ability to learn and operate new technologies, particularly those related to computers and the World Wide Web.

   RATING: (a)   (b)   (c)   (d)   (e)

8. **Being the diligent protégé of a worthy mentor**. Studying the example of an accomplished, experienced, wise person whom one admires.

   RATING: (a)   (b)   (c)   (d)   (e)

9. **Supplying focus with respect to relationships.** Approaching relationships in terms of what one has to offer others, instead of what one needs or wants from others.

   RATING: (a)   (b)   (c)   (d)   (e)

10. **Seeking out decision makers.** The ability to clarify the decisions that must be made to reach particular goals, and then to identify the individuals who have the authority to make those decisions (or the influence to affect those decisions).

   RATING: (a)   (b)   (c)   (d)   (e)

(Continued)

THE WORKER OF THE FUTURE™
PROFILE BUILDER (Continued)

11. **Total customer service mindset.** Treating everyone like a valued customer—coworkers, employees, managers, suppliers, service people, as well as actual customers. Psyching out the needs of others and seeking to address them with cheerful promptness.

    RATING: (a) (b) (c) (d) (e)

12. **Trustworthiness.** Spelling out clear expectations and assuming an absolute duty to fulfill those expectations. Being honest, realistic, responsible, on time, and accountable.

    RATING: (a) (b) (c) (d) (e)

13. **Empathy.** The ability to imagine oneself in another person's position, and to tune in to the thoughts and feelings that person might have.

    RATING: (a) (b) (c) (d) (e)

14. **Motivating others.** The ability to visualize positive results and enthusiastically share that positive vision in a way that inspires others.

    RATING: (a) (b) (c) (d) (e)

(Continued)

THE WORKER OF THE FUTURE™
PROFILE BUILDER (Continued)

15. **Facilitating the effectiveness of others.** The ability to train and coach others, set clear goals and deadlines, provide others with effective feedback, and reward good performance.

    RATING: (a) (b) (c) (d) (e)

16. **Celebrating the success of others.** Giving people credit for their achievements, no matter how small, and trying to catch people doing things right.

    RATING: (a) (b) (c) (d) (e)

17. **Being a mentor.** Helping another person learn and grow, and in the process, practicing one's leadership skills—priority setting, communication, and motivation.

    RATING: (a) (b) (c) (d) (e)

18. **Communication.** The ability to listen (or to read) carefully and understand what others are thinking, feeling, and expressing; and the ability to speak (or to write) clearly and make oneself understood.

    RATING: (a) (b) (c) (d) (e)

(Continued)

THE WORKER OF THE FUTURE™
PROFILE BUILDER (Continued)

19. **Being a great team player.** The practice of sacrificing one's own autonomy and contributing one's best ideas and hardest work to pursue a shared purpose along with others; giving up some individual recognition in order to win recognition for the group and its shared purpose.

    RATING: (a) (b) (c) (d) (e)

20. **Negotiation and conflict resolution.** The ability to clarify one's own bottom line, identify another's true bottom line, expose the common ground, and move oneself and another to that common ground.

    RATING: (a) (b) (c) (d) (e)

21. **Results focus.** The ability and inclination to organize one's work around clear, tangible goals and concrete deadlines.

    RATING: (a) (b) (c) (d) (e)

22. **Identifying opportunities to add value.** The ability to identify problems others have not identified, problems others have not solved, services and products not yet invented, or services and products in need of improvement or delivery.

    RATING: (a) (b) (c) (d) (e)

(Continued)

THE WORKER OF THE FUTURE™
PROFILE BUILDER (Continued)

23. **Seizing opportunities to add value.** The ability to identify needs, match one's skills to those needs, define the value one is capable of adding, and then create an effective sales message to persuade decision makers to authorize and/or pay for the project.

    RATING: (a) (b) (c) (d) (e)

24. **Deal closing.** The ability to clarify the parameters of a proposed transaction, identify the desired result of each party, move both parties to the common ground, eliminate mutually exclusive elements, and secure a binding agreement of both parties to execute the transaction.

    RATING: (a) (b) (c) (d) (e)

25. **Strategic planning.** The ability to plan the achievement of goals by concrete deadlines, brainstorm available sources, map out intermediate goals and deadlines, and build a schedule of daily actions to meet each intermediate goal.

    RATING: (a) (b) (c) (d) (e)

26. **Going the extra mile.** The practice of achieving more than one promises to achieve.

    RATING: (a) (b) (c) (d) (e)

(Continued)

THE WORKER OF THE FUTURE™
PROFILE BUILDER (Continued)

27. **Quality.** Holding oneself to a high standard. Thinking before speaking; outlining before writing (and always doing second drafts); planning before acting; double- and triple-checking before finalizing anything.

    RATING: (a) (b) (c) (d) (e)

28. **Integrity.** A commitment to act on one's best knowledge and intentions; to be honest with oneself and with others, and to remain faithful to basic ethical principles.

    RATING: (a) (b) (c) (d) (e)

29. **Gauging change.** The practice of monitoring feedback from every source to keep track of what is changing and what is staying the same, what is still working and what is no longer working.

    RATING: (a) (b) (c) (d) (e)

30. **Flexibility.** The willingness and ability to continually make adjustments in one's goals, plans, and practices every step of the way as necessitated by changing circumstances.

    RATING: (a) (b) (c) (d) (e)

(Continued)

THE WORKER OF THE FUTURE™
PROFILE BUILDER (Continued)

31. **Adaptability.** The ability and willingness to learn new skills, perform new tasks, do old tasks in new ways, work with new machines, new managers, new coworkers, new customers, new rules, no rules; to do whatever is needed, whenever it's needed; to go, on any given day, from one boss to another, from one team to another, from one organization to another, from one set of tasks to another.

    RATING: (a) (b) (c) (d) (e)

    _____

III. Completing the Profile

Once you have evaluated each of the thirty-one skills in terms of their importance to the position you are seeking to fill, make two lists as shown below.

List all the skills you marked as absolutely essential.

_____

_____

_____

_____

_____

(Continued)

- 28 -

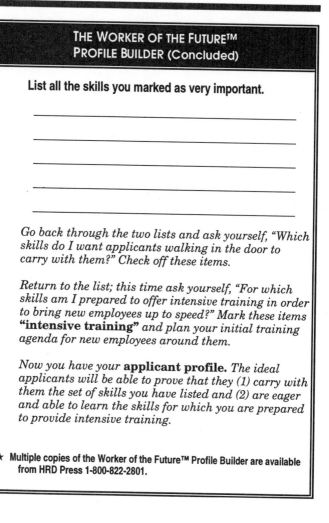

THE WORKER OF THE FUTURE™ PROFILE BUILDER (Concluded)

List all the skills you marked as very important.

_____

_____

_____

_____

_____

Go back through the two lists and ask yourself, "Which skills do I want applicants walking in the door to carry with them?" Check off these items.

Return to the list; this time ask yourself, "For which skills am I prepared to offer intensive training in order to bring new employees up to speed?" Mark these items **"intensive training"** *and plan your initial training agenda for new employees around them.*

Now you have your **applicant profile.** *The ideal applicants will be able to prove that they (1) carry with them the set of skills you have listed and (2) are eager and able to learn the skills for which you are prepared to provide intensive training.*

★ Multiple copies of the Worker of the Future™ Profile Builder are available from HRD Press 1-800-822-2801.

THE RECRUITING CAMPAIGN

*How to Attract a Large, Diverse Pool of
Applicants Who Fit the Worker Profile*

Now that you know who you are looking for, the next
step is to attract a large, diverse pool of applicants
who fit your worker profile. The best strategy is to run
your recruiting program as you would any goal-
oriented campaign:

1. Brainstorm the basics. Ask and answer some
   basic questions to clarify goals and form the
   basis of your plan.

2. Develop your recruiting plan. This includes
   generating and refining a persuasive message as
   well as planning the resources and timeline for
   delivering that message.

3. Deliver the message to the right people as
   effectively and inexpensively as possible.

4. Track results and continually revise and update
   your plan.

Part 2 gives you a full collection of tools for completing
the first two steps in a way that will both attract the
kind of applicants you want for the position and make
your entire campaign run smoothly.

Brainstorming the Basics

1. *Where may there be large concentrations of people who fit your applicant profile?*

   If you are looking for young and ambitious people in their early twenties who are sharp and eager to learn, and you are willing to deal with their possible lack of specific marketable skills, then colleges and universities will be like a gold mine for you.

   If you want people with experience in your industry, you may need to raid your competitors. Even better, re-recruit some of your former employees. You can probably find a lot of people with transferable skills, whether they have been working in industries related or unrelated to yours. (Such people can be a source of innovation because they are used to using similar skills in very different contexts and with different applications, and may see new possibilities for your organization.)

   Brainstorm answers to this question, recording them on following page.

BRAINSTORMING THE BASICS — QUESTION 1

Where may there be large concentrations of people who fit your applicant profile?

_____

_____

_____

_____

_____

_____

_____

_____

_____

_____

_____

_____

_____

_____

_____

_____

2. *For each large concentration of applicants, think of all the avenues of direct and indirect communication to that group.*

Are there opportunities to talk one to one with potential applicants? Are there intermediaries who might be helpful? For example, if you are interested in college seniors, career placement officials may be very helpful to you.

Is there a database available with the names and contact information for reaching any of the large concentrations of applicants? If not, what would it take to build one?

Are there events planned, or events you could host, that would draw large numbers of potential applicants? Are there television and radio stations, or print or Web publications, that reach many of your targets and on which you should focus paid advertising and unpaid publicity? Are there billboards anywhere on which you could post a message? What about giving away golfing shirts or mouse pads or briefcases that say *"Come work at _____ Co., the place to grow"*? (I call "extras" like that Recruiting Stuff.™)

Brainstorm answers to this question, recording them on following page.

BRAINSTORMING THE BASICS — QUESTION 2

For each large concentration of applicants, think of all the
avenues of direct and indirect communication to that group.

_____

_____

_____

_____

_____

_____

_____

_____

_____

_____

_____

_____

_____

_____

_____

_____

3. *Do you know what your target applicants are looking for in an employment relationship? If you don't, how can you find out?*

Can you conduct a poll? Organize focus groups? Hold one-to-one interviews?

Whom would you ask for information? A statistically relevant sample of individuals or small groups taken from within the applicant pool? Or some of your own employees who fit the profile?

What would you ask them? If they are looking for money? Benefits? Vacation time? Flex-time? Flex-place? Marketable skills? Exposure to decision makers? Creative challenges? Opportunities to prove themselves? Responsibility? Creative freedom? Geographical location? Varied assignments? Perks like the use of the company gym or free coffee or something similar?

You'll never know the answers to such questions for sure until you ask, and once you do, you'll probably be surprised by some of what you learn.

Brainstorm answers to this question, recording them on following page. You can add these researched items to the inventory and comparison tools you will find later in this guide.

2. The Recruiting Campaign

BRAINSTORMING THE BASICS — QUESTION 3

Do you know what your target applicants are looking for in an
employment relationship? If you don't, how can you find out?

_____

_____

_____

_____

_____

_____

_____

_____

_____

_____

_____

_____

_____

_____

_____

_____

4. *What resources are at your disposal?*

Do you have . . .

- People?
- Information?
- Knowledge?
- Materials?

- Money?
- Time?
- Space?
- Other resources?

List every resource available to you.

Brainstorm answers to this question, recording them on following page.

BRAINSTORMING THE BASICS — QUESTION 4

What resources are at your disposal?

_____

_____

_____

_____

_____

_____

_____

_____

_____

_____

_____

_____

_____

_____

_____

_____

_____

_____

Developing Your Recruiting Plan

Once you have identified (1) concentrations of people who fit your profile, (2) lines of direct and indirect communication to reach those concentrations, (3) what your targets may be looking for in an employment relationship, and (4) what resources are available to you, the basic elements for making a recruiting plan are in place.

The key to planning a successful campaign is to allocate all of your available resources to the development and effective delivery of a clear, persuasive message. Your planning approach should therefore focus on three basic tasks:

- First, **developing a persuasive message.**

- Second, **planning the delivery of the message.**

- Third, **planning a budget and timetables for executing the delivery of the message.**

This section presents a number of steps and tools designed to help you work through these tasks, including strategies and suggestions for delivering your recruiting message as effectively as possible. (Note that inventory and comparison tools can be revised to reflect your research on what target applicants want in employment relationships.)

DEVELOPING A PERSUASIVE MESSAGE

There are five steps in the development of a clear, persuasive message.

1. Conduct an inventory of all the selling points of the position for which you are hiring. Use the tool below to conduct your inventory; if necessary, revise column one to reflect your research on target applicants.

WHAT THE WORKFORCE OF THE FUTURE LOOKS FOR IN EMPLOYMENT RELATIONSHIPS	SELLING POINTS OF THE POSITION YOU HAVE TO OFFER
Marketable skills	
Relationships with decision makers	
Creative challenges	
The chance to collect proof of their ability to add value in any workplace	
Increasing spheres of responsibility	
Control over their own schedules	

2. Do some research on similar positions being offered by your competitors; using the tool below, compare your selling points to theirs.

WHAT THE WORKFORCE OF THE FUTURE LOOKS FOR	SELLING POINTS OF YOUR POSITION	SELLING POINTS OF COMPETITOR'S POSITION
Marketable skills		
Relationships with decision makers		
Creative challenges		
Proof of their ability to add value		
Increasing spheres of responsibility		
Control over their own schedules		

3. Choose a method of survey research: polling, focus groups, or one-to-one in-depth interviews.

4. Build a survey research inquiry based on comparing the selling points of your organization with the selling points of your competition. Identify which of your selling points are most effective, and provide the greatest points of contrast with those of your competition.

5. Build a clear and concise message that summarizes your best selling points, especially those that highly contrast with those of your competition.

PLANNING THE DELIVERY OF THE MESSAGE

Your first step is to identify all the media outlets you wish to use in your campaign; then you need to adopt a strategy for each outlet you have chosen, so you can use it to your optimum advantage.

Begin with the organizing tools on the next two pages. List the advertising and news outlets you are interested in, and supply related information. Suggestions for various strategies, and other useful organizing tools, are included later in this section to help you make your planning complete.

ADVERTISING OUTLET INFORMATION ORGANIZER

MEDIA OUTLET	ADVERTISING REP. & CONTACT INFORMATION (Name/Address Phone/Fax/E-Mail)	PRICE SCHEDULES	DEADLINE FOR PURCHASING ADS (No. of Days Prior to Running Ad)	DEADLINE FOR AD COPY DELIVERY (No. of Days Prior to Running Ad)

NEWS OUTLET INFORMATION ORGANIZER

MEDIA OUTLET	CONTACT (Editor, Reporter, Show Host) & CONTACT INFORMATION (Name/Address Phone/Fax/E-Mail)	DEADLINES FOR PRESS & TIMES OF BROADCAST	NOTABLE EDITORIAL POLICIES & PROCEDURES	PLATFORMS (Special Columns, Call-In Shows, On-Air Commentaries, Talk Shows, etc.)

Strategies for Delivering the Message

➡ **News strategy.** You will need to develop concrete news stories or events to pitch to editors and reporters; then you will need to write, send, and follow up a news release. These are the five key steps of the process:

1. Find an event or angle that is newsworthy. Build a list of reportable events and different news angles on your program. For example: "This year we are hiring 10 percent more employees than last year" or "We are giving out puppies to interviewees this year."

2. Write a brief news release focusing on the points you consider most newsworthy.

3. Consider assembling a news packet of photographs, documentation, or other supporting items, and send the packet with the release.

4. Send the news release (and packet if used) early enough to give a news editor time to assign a reporter to cover the story.

5. Always follow up a news release with phone calls to every person who received the release.

Use the next tool to develop your list of stories and events and to create a schedule for each one.

NEWSWORTHY STORIES AND EVENTS: LIST AND SCHEDULE

NEWS STORY OR EVENT (What makes it newsworthy?)	DATE	DEADLINE FOR DEVELOPING NEWS RELEASE & PACKET	EDITORS & REPORTERS TO RECEIVE RELEASE & PACKET	DEADLINE FOR DELIVERY OF NEWS RELEASE & PACKET	DEADLINE FOR MAKING THE FOLLOW-UP CALLS

Don't dismiss such tactics as writing letters to the editor and making calls to phone-in talk shows; these low-budget strategies can yield good results.

And don't forget that you will need a recruiting spokesperson. You should designate for this role someone internal to the organization or an outsider with name recognition and credibility with your target audience.

➡ **Paid advertising strategy.** You may want to include outside professional help when dealing with advertising, but the bottom line is, media outlets will give you lots of support with the process, as they want to make it easy for you to spend money advertising with them.

The key to creating any effective ad is being disciplined about sticking to the message. If you've done the market research and developed a powerful message, just state the message over and over again. Here are some other tips for creating ads:

• *Print ads.* When designing, use a big picture (photo or graphic) and as few words as possible (just the message and contact information). The publication's ad department will follow whatever copy and layout you specify.

- *Radio ads.* Just write a script for a 60-second time spot (read it slowly, timing yourself) and then go to the radio station. The folks there will put you in a recording studio to read the ad yourself, or, if you prefer, they will provide a voice-over person to read it. They will also add music and may have some fun suggestions.

- *Television ads.* Producing a spot can get complicated, but these days, with cable television available, it's a whole lot easier than it used to be. Your local cable vendor probably has an internal advertising department or agency that will help you buy air time and work with you on ad production, such as shooting footage and editing a 30-second spot.

   Advertising in local markets on networks like CNN, A&E, and ESPN allows you to get your message on television very inexpensively and to penetrate highly localized markets.

- *Web ads.* Advertising on the Web has the potential to be as simple as print advertising and more complex than television, but most sites that take ads will advise you on the process.

Use the following tools to organize your approach to paid media advertising.

PAID MEDIA ADVERTISING ORGANIZER

MEDIA	NUMBER OF OUTLETS FOR MEDIA	BUDGET FOR MEDIA	TIME FRAME IN WHICH TO ADVERTISE
Print			
Radio			
Television			
Web			

PRINT ADVERTISING-BUYING ORGANIZER

NEWSPAPER OR MAGAZINE	DATES	SIZE OF AD (in square inches)	TOTAL NO. OF ADS	COST PER AD	TOTAL COST PER PRINT SOURCE	RUNNING TOTAL

RADIO ADVERTISING-BUYING ORGANIZER

STATION	START DATE	END DATE	NO. ADS TOTAL	NO. ADS PER DAY	COST PER AD	TOTAL COST PER STATION	RUNNING TOTAL

TELEVISION ADVERTISING-BUYING ORGANIZER

NETWORK	START DATE	END DATE	NO. ADS TOTAL	NO. ADS PER DAY	COST PER AD	TOTAL COST PER NETWORK	RUNNING TOTAL

WEB ADVERTISING-BUYING ORGANIZER

Web site	Start Date	End Date	No. Ads Total	Ad Content & Format	Cost Per Ad	Total Cost Per Site	Running Total

➡ **Direct contact strategy.** There are five possible methods for directly contacting your target applicants: telephone, fax, mail, e-mail, and person-to-person meetings.

The key to any effective direct contact strategy is being in control of a database with the correct contact information. So first, identify and secure available databases with contact information. Second, decide how many people you'll need to contact in order to attract the desired number of applicants (try to contact at least 100 times the number you are seeking). Third, decide what means of direct contact will best help you reach those people. Here are some useful tips:

- *Telephone.* You can build a team of callers to phone potential applicants and let them know about the career opportunity you have to offer. Or you can hire a phone bank.

- *Fax.* This is an inexpensive way to get printed information in front of people. Faxing is not always good for "headhunting" though, for some constituencies are hard to reach by fax and many faxes are not secure.

- *Mail.* You can send personal letters, glossy foldout brochures, or simple postcards. You may want to handle the mailing yourself. Or you may prefer to contract out to a direct-mail firm.

- *E-mail.* This form of communication is very personal, so be careful about imposing. You might consider sending a mass e-mail inviting people to visit a special recruiting Web site.

- *Person-to-person meetings.* The best way to meet personally with people is to participate in or host an event that draws a crowd of potential applicants (see the Event Organizer on the next page).

No matter what form of direct contact you choose, consider including a giveaway item with your recruiting message on it. Everybody enjoys getting "stuff" (again, I like to call such extras Recruiting Stuff™; note that we at Rainmaker, Inc., have a good selection of Recruiting Stuff™ available).

The first tool that follows, the Event Organizer, provides you with a handy framework for your event planning. The second tool, the Direct Contact Organizer, helps you project your strategy month by month; simply log the number and type of people you want to contact, then mark the form(s) of contact you plan to use and note any relevant information.

EVENT ORGANIZER

PARTICULARS	PERSON RESPONSIBLE	DEADLINE
The place		
The date		
Food, beverage, or other refreshments		
Entertainment or programming		
Invitation list		
Design, printing, and mailing of invitations		
Follow-up calls to those invited		
Plan for delivering the message		

DIRECT CONTACT ORGANIZER *(January to June)*

Month	How many people? Which people? From what database?	Phone	Fax	Mail	E-Mail	Events
Jan.						
Feb.						
March						
April						
May						
June						

DIRECT CONTACT ORGANIZER *(July to December)*

Month	HOW MANY PEOPLE? WHICH PEOPLE? FROM WHAT DATABASE?	PHONE	FAX	MAIL	E-MAIL	EVENTS
July						
Aug.						
Sept.						
Oct.						
Nov.						
Dec.						

➡ **Visibility and awareness strategy.** If you don't want to buy advertising, to generate news stories, or to blast your potential applicants with phone calls, faxes, mail, e-mail, or events, you might consider running an all-out visibility campaign to raise your target group awareness of what your organization offers as an employer.

You can increase visibility through the use of signs, billboards, and bumper stickers (ask your employees to put the stickers on their cars) and by giving away Recruiting Stuff.™

PLANNING A BUDGET AND TIMETABLES

Finally, you will need to plan a recruiting budget and timetables for executing the delivery of the message. The next two organizing tools are designed to help you get through this last planning step as easily and effectively as possible.

The Recruiting Budget Planner lists expense items and gives you room to record the total amount for each item and the date when expenditures will be made. With the Timetable of Campaign Activities, you can project when the recruiting message will be developed and then log, month by month, the ongoing strategies you will use to deliver that message.

RECRUITING BUDGET PLANNER

Items of Expense	Total Amount	When Expenditures Will Be Made
1. *Administrative costs:* personnel, equipment, utilities, & supplies		
2. *Database acquisition, tailoring, & maintenance*		
3. *Survey research:* polling, focus groups, or in-depth interviews		
4. *Mailing material:* letters, brochures, postcards, & postage		
5. *Telephone, fax, e-mail:* phone bills & other costs; or costs of outsource phonebank or broadcast fax or e-mail services		
6. *Paid advertising budget:* per se ad costs (cost times placement) plus production costs or cost of using advertising professionals		
7. *News strategy:* possible costs of staging events or involving paid spokespeople or professional public relations people		
8. *Visibility materials:* cost of signs, billboards, & materials such as Recruiting Stuff™		

TIMETABLE OF CAMPAIGN ACTIVITIES *(January to June)*

MONTH	MESSAGE DEVELOPMENT	NEWS	PAID ADVERTISING	DIRECT CONTACT	VISIBILITY
Jan.					
Feb.					
March					
April					
May					
June					

TIMETABLE OF CAMPAIGN ACTIVITIES *(July to December)*

MONTH	MESSAGE DEVELOPMENT	NEWS	PAID ADVERTISING	DIRECT CONTACT	VISIBILITY
July					
Aug.					
Sept.					
Oct.					
Nov.					
Dec.					

Once you have planned your strategies for delivering the recruiting message, it's time to move into action and get the campaign underway. Always track your results and continually revise and update your plan.

EXTRAS TO KEEP IN MIND

Want to improve your campaign? Try these tips.

Six Quick Tips to Improve Your Recruiting Campaign

★ Gear your Web site to recruiting, since potential applicants will visit more often than potential clients and customers.

★ Encourage your best employees to recruit their friends.

★ Build a personal relationship with college placement officials so they send you their best people.

★ Discuss career issues with your favorite clients, customers, and vendors, and let them know about the opportunities in your organization.

★ Provide internships in order to preview potential recruits and to give them a preview of your organization.

★ Stay in close touch with prized employees—an ounce of retention is worth a pound of recruiting.

Another possibility is to use a new kind of recruiting service that benefits employers and young talent alike. These services offer electronic databases of résumés and job-postings that can be searched, respectively, by recruiters and job-seekers. Go out on the Web and search among thousands of great résumés to build an applicant pool quickly and efficiently.

Here are three such services.

Cutting-Edge Recruiting Services

★ **JobDirect** currently has more than 40,000 student members looking for jobs and projects, and the service predicts it will soon have more than 80,000 members.

This is probably the best source of résumés from potential applicants. Companies are also invited to post openings on JobDirect.

Contact Information:

> WEB: http://www.jobdirect.com
>
> PHONE: (203) 629-2201
>
> CONTACT PERSON: Rachel Bell

★ **College Central Network** is a recruiting service similar to JobDirect; however, whereas JobDirect emphasizes the résumé databases

available for employers to search through,
College Central Network emphasizes the
opportunity for employers to post job openings
that students can search through.

Contact Information:

> WEB: http://www.collegecentral.com
>
> PHONE: (800) 442-3614
>
> CONTACT PERSON: Stuart Nachbar

★ **CareerPath.com** is the employment Web site
that lists help wanted ads from major market
newspapers and claims to be the most searched,
most trafficked job site on the Web. According to
Yahoo! Internet Life, CareerPath.com is the
largest database of current jobs.

Contact Information:

> WEB: http://www.careerpath.com
>
> PHONE: (213) 623-0200
>
> CONTACT PERSON: Gail Crowe

★ **Multiple copies of the *Worker of the
Future™ Recruiting Campaign Planner* are
available from HRD Press. 1-800-822-2801.**

PART 3

SELECTING THE STARS OF THE WORKFORCE OF THE FUTURE

Profiling and attracting applicants are the most important elements in the selection process. If you have planned and are executing an effective recruiting campaign, you will have a lot of applicants to choose from. If you have given thorough attention to profiling the ideal applicant for the position, then the selection process will mainly focus on determining which applicants best fit the profile.

The Old-Fashioned Approach

In the workplace of the past, your goal was to hire long-term employees—people who would join the corporate family, hitch their wagons to your star, pay their dues, and climb the ladder. You were looking for people you might like to work with for the next thirty years or so, and the process of selecting them was fairly straightforward.

In that process, applicants would be expected to send in a cover letter with a résumé and then wait to hear from you. If the résumé indicated a sufficient background in education and experience, you would call the applicant to schedule an initial interview. If the applicant passed muster, you called him or her back for an extensive set of interviews with some key decision makers and you probably asked for a letter of reference from a previous employer.

Times have changed, and so have hiring goals and the selection process.

Selecting Value Adders in the Workplace of the Future

Today you are not looking for people to join the family and climb the corporate ladder; rather, you need people who bring specific skills to the table—who can get up to speed quickly and start making valuable contributions right away. The old selection practices simply don't address this need very well.

Cover letters can be misleading, and although résumés are useful to some degree, they don't tell you everything you need to know about a person. Plus you can get lost in a pile of cover letters and résumés without ever determining who stands out from the crowd. Interviews are not as reliable as they used to be, because so many people are practicing how to give the "right" answers in job interviews—the kind of answers "interviewers want to hear." And you can't trust letters of reference because everybody is afraid of getting sued.

To select the value adders best suited to contribute to the workplace of the future, you need *good, solid proof* that applicants have the skills they need to get up to speed quickly and start contributing right away *and* that applicants are prepared to learn the skills for which you are prepared to provide intensive training. How to get that proof is the focus of Part 3.

Getting the Proof You Need: Methods and Tools

There are four basic methods that, when used in tandem, will update your selection process and produce the kind of evidence you need to select the best applicant for the position you want to fill.

1. *Collect detailed proposals*, in addition to résumés. Limit the use of résumés to building a large, diverse applicant pool (consider using electronic databases as explained in Part 2). For your current purpose, you need detailed proposals outlining exactly how the applicant intends to add value in your organization.

2. *Focus interviews on concrete skills*, not long-term employment requirements (e.g., whether you'd like to work with the person for the next

thirty years). Orient your interviews around the
skills you need applicants to carry with them
and the skills you need applicants to learn.

3. *Collect "free samples" of applicant achievements*,
in addition to references. You want tangible
proof that an applicant's ability matches his or
her claims. This requires asking the applicant
for results that you can see firsthand, rather
than reading about them in less-than-
trustworthy references.

4. *Provide job previews*, not only job descriptions.
Instead of risking a bad fit, insist on giving
finalists extensive and realistic previews of the
job so they know exactly what the job entails.
Make sure you get proof that the person you
select has no illusions and won't be giving his or
her notice after only a few days on the job.

More about each method follows, along with tools and
suggestions for carrying out the four methods to your
optimum advantage.

Collecting Detailed Proposals

Your request for applicant proposals should be clear and specific:

> *"Submit a detailed proposal outlining exactly how you intend to add value in our organization."*

You may want to leave the request at that and see what applicants come up with on their own. The response you get will tell you a lot about the resourcefulness of your applicants and allow you to gauge their perceptions of your needs, their skills, and the potential marriage between your needs and their skills.

An alternative approach is to give applicants some guidance in creating the proposals. The following tool, Applicant Proposal Guidelines, is designed for this purpose. To use the tool, you must provide applicants with a description of your organization's needs. Record your description in the first response box. Again, be clear and specific: applicants will be asked to base their responses on your description, and they must have a good idea of what the organization's needs entail.

APPLICANT PROPOSAL GUIDELINES

Our organization has the following needs:

1. Please describe your skills as they address the needs above.

2. Please let us know how you intend to apply your skills to address the needs described above. (Exactly what do you intend to do? How? Why?)

(Continued)

APPLICANT PROPOSAL GUIDELINES (Concluded)

3. Please propose a timetable of concrete goals and deadlines.

GOALS	DEADLINES

Focusing Interviews on Concrete Skills

Too many employers conduct interviews that are vague and unfocused or, even worse, focused on irrelevant or inappropriate subject matter. I've heard stories about interviewers asking inappropriate questions like "Do you intend to have children?" or stupid questions like "What can you tell me in the next sixty seconds that will really impress me?"

A surprising number of interviewers simply read an applicant's résumé aloud (probably reading it for the first time), pausing to ask for amplification here and clarification there. Many just want to "get to know the applicant" by chatting about sports or clothes or classes the applicant took in college. Some outright waste the interview by doing all the talking themselves.

Focus interviews on the skills you want applicants to carry in the door and the skills you want them to be prepared to learn. The following interviewing tool—based on the Thirty-One Skills to Look for in Workers of the Future—will help you. If you are conducting in-person interviews, use the questions that focus on the skills you have identified in your applicant profile. If you are interviewing applicants on paper, either via mail or e-mail, or on-site, ask them to complete the entire interview.

WORKER OF THE FUTURE™
DO-IT-YOURSELF INTERVIEW

Everyone has different strengths and weaknesses. We are asking you to rate yourself on thirty-one skills and let us know what you perceive as your strengths and weaknesses.

We are also interested in knowing why you have selected your particular ratings and are asking you to provide explanations and examples.

For each skill, please take these steps:

*1. Carefully read through the skill; then circle **one or two ratings** based on the following scale:*

(a) This is one of my greatest strengths.

(b) My confidence with this skill is high, but I am stronger on other skills.

(c) I am eager to go through intensive training on this skill.

(d) This is not one of my strengths, and I would not choose to go through intensive training on this skill.

(e) This is an area where I am weak and I know it.

2. Explain your answer in the space provided. Be sure to include examples.

(Continued)

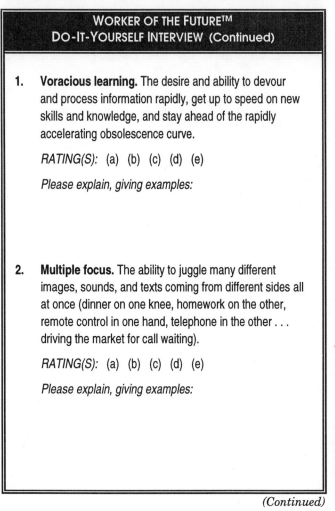

WORKER OF THE FUTURE™
DO-IT-YOURSELF INTERVIEW (Continued)

1. **Voracious learning.** The desire and ability to devour and process information rapidly, get up to speed on new skills and knowledge, and stay ahead of the rapidly accelerating obsolescence curve.

    RATING(S): (a) (b) (c) (d) (e)

    Please explain, giving examples:

2. **Multiple focus.** The ability to juggle many different images, sounds, and texts coming from different sides all at once (dinner on one knee, homework on the other, remote control in one hand, telephone in the other . . . driving the market for call waiting).

    RATING(S): (a) (b) (c) (d) (e)

    Please explain, giving examples:

(Continued)

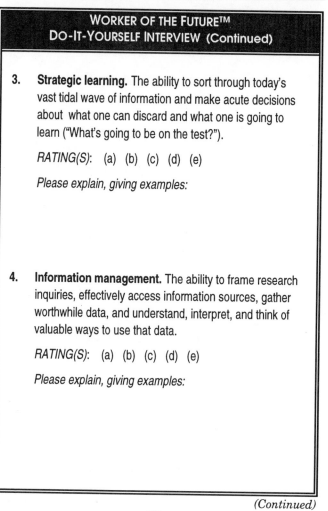

WORKER OF THE FUTURE™
DO-IT-YOURSELF INTERVIEW (Continued)

3. **Strategic learning.** The ability to sort through today's vast tidal wave of information and make acute decisions about what one can discard and what one is going to learn ("What's going to be on the test?").

    RATING(S): (a) (b) (c) (d) (e)

    Please explain, giving examples:

4. **Information management.** The ability to frame research inquiries, effectively access information sources, gather worthwhile data, and understand, interpret, and think of valuable ways to use that data.

    RATING(S): (a) (b) (c) (d) (e)

    Please explain, giving examples:

(Continued)

WORKER OF THE FUTURE™
DO-IT-YOURSELF INTERVIEW (Continued)

5. **Critical thinking.** The ability to differentiate between reliable and unreliable information, to carefully weigh the strengths of conflicting views, and to make reasoned judgments. The habit of taking the time to consider possibilities, and not become attached to one point of view. Balancing an openness to others' views with independent judgment.

    RATING(S): (a) (b) (c) (d) (e)

    Please explain, giving examples:

6. **Cultural literacy.** The desire and ability to master foreign languages and foreign cultures and to operate successfully in a global marketplace.

    RATING(S): (a) (b) (c) (d) (e)

    Please explain, giving examples:

(Continued)

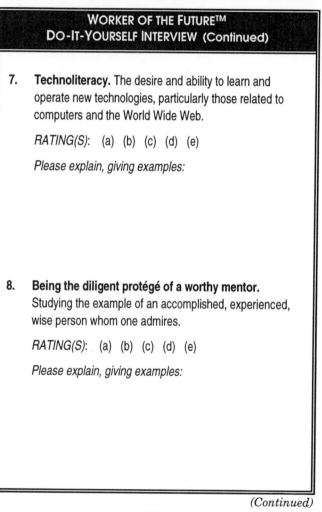

WORKER OF THE FUTURE™
DO-IT-YOURSELF INTERVIEW (Continued)

7. **Technoliteracy.** The desire and ability to learn and operate new technologies, particularly those related to computers and the World Wide Web.

   RATING(S): (a) (b) (c) (d) (e)

   Please explain, giving examples:

8. **Being the diligent protégé of a worthy mentor.** Studying the example of an accomplished, experienced, wise person whom one admires.

   RATING(S): (a) (b) (c) (d) (e)

   Please explain, giving examples:

(Continued)

9. **Supply focus with respect to relationships.**
Approaching relationships in terms of what one has to
offer others, instead of what one needs or wants from
others.

RATING(S): (a) (b) (c) (d) (e)

Please explain, giving examples:

10. **Seeking out decision makers.** The ability to clarify the
decisions that must be made to reach particular goals,
and then to identify the individuals who have the authority
to make those decisions (or the influence to affect those
decisions).

RATING(S): (a) (b) (c) (d) (e)

Please explain, giving examples:

(Continued)

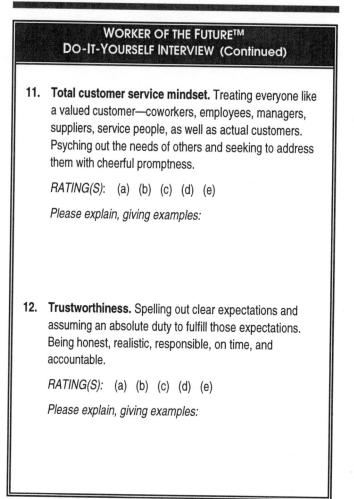

WORKER OF THE FUTURE™
DO-IT-YOURSELF INTERVIEW (Continued)

11. **Total customer service mindset.** Treating everyone like a valued customer—coworkers, employees, managers, suppliers, service people, as well as actual customers. Psyching out the needs of others and seeking to address them with cheerful promptness.

    RATING(S): (a) (b) (c) (d) (e)

    Please explain, giving examples:

12. **Trustworthiness.** Spelling out clear expectations and assuming an absolute duty to fulfill those expectations. Being honest, realistic, responsible, on time, and accountable.

    RATING(S): (a) (b) (c) (d) (e)

    Please explain, giving examples:

(Continued)

WORKER OF THE FUTURE™
DO-IT-YOURSELF INTERVIEW (Continued)

13. **Empathy.** The ability to imagine oneself in another person's position, and to tune in to the thoughts and feelings that person might have.

    RATING(S):   (a) (b) (c) (d) (e)

    Please explain, giving examples:

14. **Motivating others.** The ability to visualize positive results and enthusiastically share that positive vision in a way that inspires others.

    RATING(S):   (a) (b) (c) (d) (e)

    Please explain, giving examples:

(Continued)

WORKER OF THE FUTURE™
DO-IT-YOURSELF INTERVIEW (Continued)

15. **Facilitating the effectiveness of others.** The ability to train and coach others, set clear goals and deadlines, provide others with effective feedback, and reward good performance.

    RATING(S): (a) (b) (c) (d) (e)

    Please explain, giving examples:

16. **Celebrating the success of others.** Giving people credit for their achievements, no matter how small, and trying to catch people doing things right.

    RATING(S): (a) (b) (c) (d) (e)

    Please explain, giving examples:

(Continued)

– 83 –

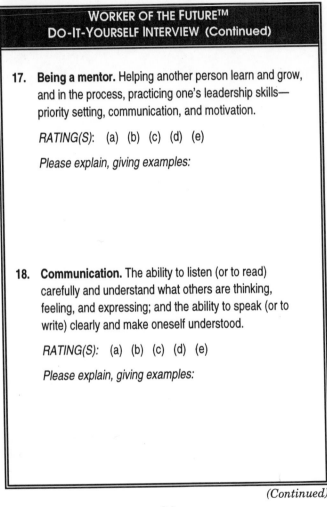

WORKER OF THE FUTURE™
DO-IT-YOURSELF INTERVIEW (Continued)

17. **Being a mentor.** Helping another person learn and grow, and in the process, practicing one's leadership skills—priority setting, communication, and motivation.

    RATING(S): (a) (b) (c) (d) (e)

    Please explain, giving examples:

18. **Communication.** The ability to listen (or to read) carefully and understand what others are thinking, feeling, and expressing; and the ability to speak (or to write) clearly and make oneself understood.

    RATING(S): (a) (b) (c) (d) (e)

    Please explain, giving examples:

(Continued)

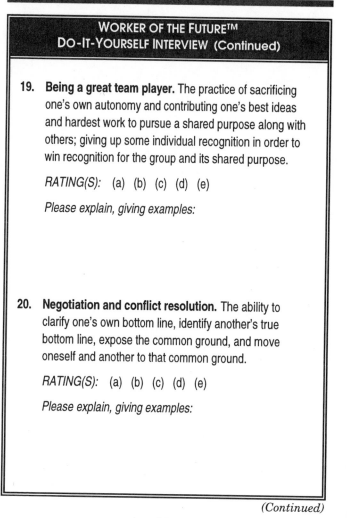

WORKER OF THE FUTURE™
DO-IT-YOURSELF INTERVIEW (Continued)

19. **Being a great team player.** The practice of sacrificing one's own autonomy and contributing one's best ideas and hardest work to pursue a shared purpose along with others; giving up some individual recognition in order to win recognition for the group and its shared purpose.

   RATING(S): (a) (b) (c) (d) (e)

   Please explain, giving examples:

20. **Negotiation and conflict resolution.** The ability to clarify one's own bottom line, identify another's true bottom line, expose the common ground, and move oneself and another to that common ground.

   RATING(S): (a) (b) (c) (d) (e)

   Please explain, giving examples:

(Continued)

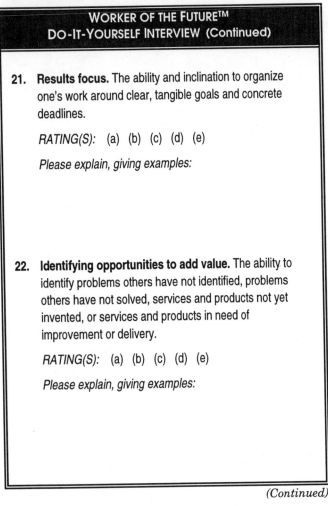

WORKER OF THE FUTURE™
DO-IT-YOURSELF INTERVIEW (Continued)

21. **Results focus.** The ability and inclination to organize one's work around clear, tangible goals and concrete deadlines.

    RATING(S): (a) (b) (c) (d) (e)

    Please explain, giving examples:

22. **Identifying opportunities to add value.** The ability to identify problems others have not identified, problems others have not solved, services and products not yet invented, or services and products in need of improvement or delivery.

    RATING(S): (a) (b) (c) (d) (e)

    Please explain, giving examples:

(Continued)

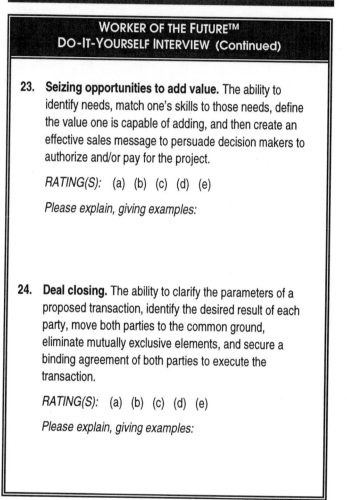

WORKER OF THE FUTURE™
DO-IT-YOURSELF INTERVIEW (Continued)

23. **Seizing opportunities to add value.** The ability to identify needs, match one's skills to those needs, define the value one is capable of adding, and then create an effective sales message to persuade decision makers to authorize and/or pay for the project.

    RATING(S): (a) (b) (c) (d) (e)

    Please explain, giving examples:

24. **Deal closing.** The ability to clarify the parameters of a proposed transaction, identify the desired result of each party, move both parties to the common ground, eliminate mutually exclusive elements, and secure a binding agreement of both parties to execute the transaction.

    RATING(S): (a) (b) (c) (d) (e)

    Please explain, giving examples:

(Continued)

25. **Strategic planning.** The ability to plan the achievement of goals by concrete deadlines, brainstorm available sources, map out intermediate goals and deadlines, and build a schedule of daily actions to meet each intermediate goal.

    RATING(S): (a) (b) (c) (d) (e)

    Please explain, giving examples:

26. **Going the extra mile.** The practice of achieving more than one promises to achieve.

    RATING(S): (a) (b) (c) (d) (e)

    Please explain, giving examples:

(Continued)

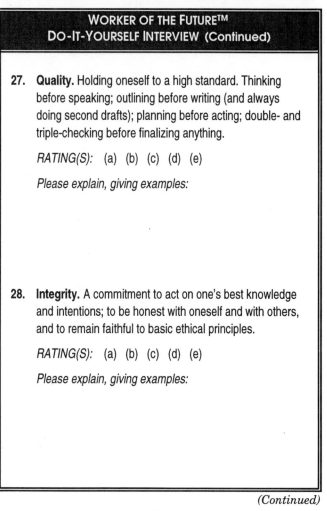

WORKER OF THE FUTURE™
DO-IT-YOURSELF INTERVIEW (Continued)

27. **Quality.** Holding oneself to a high standard. Thinking before speaking; outlining before writing (and always doing second drafts); planning before acting; double- and triple-checking before finalizing anything.

RATING(S): (a) (b) (c) (d) (e)

Please explain, giving examples:

28. **Integrity.** A commitment to act on one's best knowledge and intentions; to be honest with oneself and with others, and to remain faithful to basic ethical principles.

RATING(S): (a) (b) (c) (d) (e)

Please explain, giving examples:

(Continued)

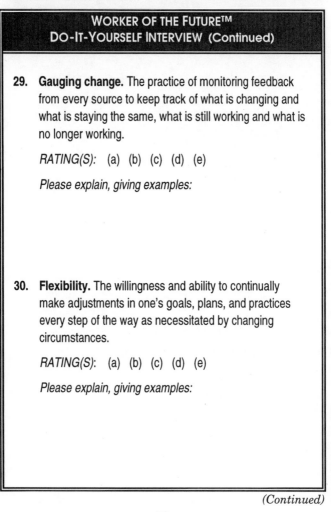

WORKER OF THE FUTURE™
DO-IT-YOURSELF INTERVIEW (Continued)

29. **Gauging change.** The practice of monitoring feedback from every source to keep track of what is changing and what is staying the same, what is still working and what is no longer working.

    RATING(S): (a) (b) (c) (d) (e)

    Please explain, giving examples:

30. **Flexibility.** The willingness and ability to continually make adjustments in one's goals, plans, and practices every step of the way as necessitated by changing circumstances.

    RATING(S): (a) (b) (c) (d) (e)

    Please explain, giving examples:

(Continued)

WORKER OF THE FUTURE™
DO-IT-YOURSELF INTERVIEW (Concluded)

31. **Adaptability.** The ability and willingness to learn new skills, perform new tasks, do old tasks in new ways, work with new machines, new managers, new coworkers, new customers, new rules, no rules; to do whatever is needed, whenever it's needed; to go, on any given day, from one boss to another, from one team to another, from one organization to another, from one set of tasks to another.

RATING(S):   (a) (b) (c) (d) (e)

Please explain, giving examples:

ANALYZING THE DO-IT-YOURSELF INTERVIEW

The key to analyzing the interview is to remember that it revolves around self-assessment: you have asked your applicants to rate themselves and explain themselves in terms of the Thirty-One Skills to Look for in Workers of the Future™—the same set of skills used in the Profile Builder™ and on which your applicant profile is based.

Ultimately, you only need to evaluate how well each applicant fits your applicant profile. Return to the profile and focus your evaluation on the interview questions that correspond to the required skills as indicated in the profile. Study applicants' self-evaluations for those required skills, looking closely at the explanations and examples that back up those self-evaluations.

★ Multiple copies of the Worker of the Future™
Do-It-Yourself Interview
are available from HRD Press 1-800-822-2801

Collecting "Free Samples" of Applicant Achievements

The best indication of the kind of work a person is going to do for you is evidence of the kind of work they have done for others (or themselves). Ask applicants to provide you with some tangible results—samples of work they have done—and make sure you can verify that the work was done by the applicant.

Tangible results will come in all shapes and sizes, depending on the applicant's work experience. If the applicant has experience as a writer, ask for a writing sample. If the applicant has experience as a musician, request a song. If he or she has experience as a teacher, ask to see a former student or to look over student evaluations. If the applicant has experience in customer service, ask to see a satisfied customer or a customer service award, or ask the applicant to serve a customer while you watch. If he or she has been an auditor, request an audit report. And so on.

Remember to keep focused on the position you want to fill and the kind of experience appropriate to that position. Collect only the type of samples that will truly help you find the right person for the position.

Providing Job Previews

One of the most common causes of voluntary turnover is disillusionment on the part of new employees when they find out that the job they were hired to do is not exactly what they envisioned when they applied for it. This problem can be remedied if you make sure that, once you select applicants who seem most suitable for the position, you give them an accurate preview of the actual day-to-day experience of accomplishing the required job tasks and responsibilities. Moreover, job previews will often allow you to get one final look at applicants in the context of the work you are hiring them to do.

Here are five ways to provide a job preview:

1. Offer the applicant the opportunity to "tag along" with another employee who is doing the same (or a similar) job. By tagging along for several days, a week, or more, your applicant will get a good picture of what the job actually entails.

2. Offer internships to potential applicants.

3. Produce a videotape, an audiotape, or a CD-ROM of employees performing the key

tasks and responsibilities of the job; then give applicants an opportunity to review what you have produced.

4. Create a print document to achieve results similar to those in the previous method but at a lower cost; then give applicants a chance to review the written document.

5. Encourage applicants to engage in frank discussions with you or your employers about the low points, as well as the high points, of the position you are seeking to fill.

CONCLUSION

If you need flexible, technoliterate, information savvy workers who think like entrepreneurs, take charge of their own careers, and stand ready to adapt themselves to everchanging roles and responsibilities, the Generation X workforce is a perfect match. Young skilled workers are in great demand, however, and consistently recruiting the best requires a new approach as well as a serious commitment.

Discard obsolete criteria from the workplace of the past and use the thirty-one skills outlined in Part 1 to build a skill-based profile relevant to the workplace of the future.

Use the planning tools in Part 2 to create a full-scale recruiting campaign, so you have a large diverse applicant pool from which to choose.

Once you have a large pool from which to choose, Part 3 will help you select the applicants who have the skills you need.

I hope you will follow this new approach and transform today's staffing crisis into a strategic advantage by becoming the employer of choice for Generation X in your industry.

INDEX

NOTES

NOTES

NOTES

NOTES

NOTES